The
Awesome
TRAVEL TRIVIA
Book

365 weird, random but interesting
Geography and **World** fun facts

by **Iwiz from Smart Impact**

About Iwiz

 **Iwiz** arrived on **Earth** a few years ago as a space tourist to witness a very special cosmic event : a **solar eclipse**. He was so amazed by what he saw that he decided to stay for a while and learn everything he could about our planet and its inhabitants.

Obviously, he became fascinated with one specific species : **humans**. He started studying our different cultures, our food, our languages, our History. He traveled all around the world to meet us (in disguise, of course) and interact with us.

After a few years, he wanted to share his wisdom with everyone and started writing **books** about all the knowledge he gathered.

In particular, "The **Awesome TRAVEL TRiViA** Book" is a collection of fun facts about the wonderful act of **traveling**. You'll learn about **weird hotels**, crazy airlines rules and also get to know hidden facts about world famous tourist attractions.

Join the Mothership !

If you like my **books**, there is a big chance you'll like my **newsletter**.

You'll regularly receive **special fun facts**, links to **articles** I found really interesting online and even **quizzes** to test your general knowledge.

I'll also keep you updated on new book release and free book promotion events I will be running.

So let's join the **Smart Impact Mothership** !

To **sign up** just scan this **QR code** –>

or simply type this URL : **smartimpact.space/ newsletter**

The Awesome TRAVEL TRIVIA Book
by Iwiz from Smart Impact

1.

Every **60 seconds**, around **2,000 people** land in a foreign country.

2.

A quarter of UK holidaymakers take **BRITISH tea bags** with them when they go abroad.

3.

Since the **1990s**, it is illegal to eat **chewing gum** in **SINGAPORE**.

4.

Currently only **five countries** in the **world** don't have any **airport** : ANDORRA, LIECHTENSTEIN, MONACO, SAN MARINO and VATICAN CITY.

5.

You can kind of step back **seven to eight years** in time when you visit ETHIOPIA, as they follow a different calendar than most of the **world**.

6.

There is enough **fuel** in a **Boeing 747 plane** to make **4 trips around the world** with a **car**.

7.

The **Dry valleys** of **Antartica** have not seen a drop of rain or snow for **2 million years**.

8.

The **world map** we are most familiar with was actually invented to guide **sailors**. If you trace a straight line between **two ports** and follow that direction with your **boat**, you'll end up exactly at your **final destination**.

9.

The people of the **NETHERLANDS** drink the most **coffee** with around **2.5 cups per person per day**.

10.

"**Machu Picchu**" means "**Old Mountain**" in Quechua, an ancient **PERUVIAN** language.

11.

The **FRENCH-SWISS** border runs directly through the **Hotel Arbez**.

12.

Some **little shops** in the middle of the **Swiss Alps** are left unattended and function with an honor system. **Clients** just leave their money in a little basket.

13.

The first **hotel reservation system** was established in **1947**.

14.

One **Airbus A380**, biggest commercial **plane** in the **world**, has **330 miles (530 km)** of electrical cables.

15.

The country of **LESOTHO** is completely inside the country of **SOUTH AFRICA**.

16.

Twenty-one of the **world**'s **twenty-five** most venomous **snakes** are indigenous to **AUSTRALIA**.

17.

The largest hotel in the **world** is the **First World Hotel** in **MALAYSIA** with **7,351 rooms** divided between two buildings.

18.

Passports didn't have **photographs** before **WWI** but it changed because during the war, a **German spy** successfully entered the **UK** with someone else's **U.S.** passport.

19.

KLM, established in **1919**, is the **world**'s oldest airline still in operation.

20.

One of the earliest mentions of a paperwork used for safe passage (ancestor of the **passport**) can be seen in the **Bible** dating around **450 BC**.

21.

Chicken Tikka Masala was invented in **GLASGOW, SCOTLAND**.

22.

The flag of **MOZAMBiQUE** is the only one to display a modern assault rifle, the **AK-47**.

23.

In **Avanos Hair Museum**, **TURKEY**, you can find the **world**'s largest collection of **hair** donated by more than **16,000 women** from all over the **world**.

24.

Despite its name, **Mount Augustus**, **AUSTRALIA** is not a **mountain** but the biggest rock in the **world**. It is over **2620 ft. (800 m)** high and can be seen from a distance of **93 miles (150 km)**.

25.

During flights, the changing air pressure numbs about **one-third** of a person's **taste buds**. That's why airlines add **spices** to the food they serve.

26.

Around **50,000 dead bodies** are transported by **airplane** every year.

27.

At **Tallin Airport**, ESTONiA, there is a library where you can borrow books for your trip and the whole thing operates purely on trust.

28.

LiBYA is the country with the highest percentage of deserts in the **world** (**99% of its territory**).

29.

$3,500 worth of coins are thrown every day for good luck in the **Trevi fountain** in **ROMA**, **ITALY**.

30.

In **SOUTH KOREA**, each year, there is a special day called **Suneung** where everyone is silent to help students focus for the most important exam of their life.

31.

MAWSYNRAM, **INDIA** is the wettest place on **Earth**. It receives, on average, **724 in. (18.38 m)** of rain each year.

32.

It is not unusual to see **24/7 restaurants** in the **UNITED STATES**.

33.

Credit cards were first invented by **hotels** in the **1920s**.

34.

The word "**passport**" comes from two old **FRENCH** words "**passer**" and "**port/porte**" which mean "**to pass through a port/ door**". It's unclear if it was at first referring to a **sea port** or to the **gates of a city**.

35.

It took **14 years** to carve the presidential faces on **Mount Rushmore** in the **UNITED STATES.**

36.

There is an annex of the **Rijksmuseum**, one of the very best art museums in the **world**, at **Schiphol Amsterdam Airport** in the **NETHERLANDS.**

37.

The **SPANISH** people were the first **Europeans** to use tomatoes to make their sauces.

38.

NACO, Arizona and **NACO**, MEXiCO were once part of the same city but are now separated by the **U.S.-Mexican border**. Every year, a volleyball game is played between both cities over the border fence.

39.

The **Burj Khalifa** in **DUBAi** is the tallest building in the **world** (over **2716 ft. or 828 m high**). It's almost **three times** higher than the **Eiffel Tower** in **PARiS**.

40.

GiETHOORN, a small village of the **NETHERLANDS**, has no streets, only water canals.

41.

A **Boeing 747** is made up of **6 million parts**.

42.

Many of the stones used to build **Machu Picchu, PERU** exceed **110,000 lbs (50 tons)**.

43.

The brightest **light** in the **world** is shot towards the sky from the **Luxor Las Vegas hotel**. It can be seen up to **275 mi. (443 km)** away.

44.

Wearing any **uniform** is forbidden on a **passport photo.**

45.

The flag of **SOUTH SUDAN** is older than the country itself, it was adopted in **2005** while the country only became independent in **2011.**

46.

It's considered rude to tip **waiters** in **SOUTH KOREA.**

47.

In **MOSCOW**, **RUSSiA**, **stray dogs** have learned to commute from the **suburbs** to the **city** to scavenge for food then go back home.

48.

Passengers can enjoy live concerts at six different stages at **Nashville International Airport, USA**.

49.

We found archeological traces of **camping tents** during the **Stone Age**. They were dated from around **40,000 BC**.

50.

There is a free public **wine fountain** in the small town of **ORTONA**, **ITALY**.

51.

Once a year, **BOLIVIANS** hide **coins** in **cakes**. Whoever finds the money is said to have very good luck for **the rest of the year**.

52.

One third (over 13,000) of the **world's airports** are located in the **UNITED STATES**.

53.

The first online check-in facility was introduced by **Alaskan Airlines** in **1999**.

54.

In **LATViA**, people avoid giving **socks** or **shoes** as a gift. It's because there is a superstition saying that would cause the **recipient** to walk out of their life.

55.

In **DENMARK,** if you are still single on your **25th birthday**, the tradition is to throw **cinnamon** at you.

56.

Some **cruise ships** have an on-board jail called a brig.

57.

The busiest **train station** in the **world** is **Shinjuku station** in **TOKYO**, **JAPAN** with over **3.6 million daily passengers**.

58.

The longest **passenger flight** without any stopover is **SiNGAPORE – NEW YORK** with almost **19 hours**.

59.

Disneyland California is the most photographed place in the **world**.

60.

On the island of **Yap**, a state of **MiCRONESiA**, **rocks** are still used as currency.

61.

FRANCE covers **12 different timezones**, more than any country on the planet thanks to its **overseas territories**.

62.

195 countries are officially recognized by the **United Nations**.

63.

To this day, you can still see the division between **East** and **West Germany** due to different **light bulb colors.**

64.

The number that designates an **airport runway** is not random. It corresponds to its geographical orientation like on a **compass.** This design helps **pilots** land by assigning them the **runway** with the most favorable wind orientation.

65.

In **JAPAN**, napping at work is not only permitted but even encouraged since it's a sign of hard work.

66.

SAN MARINO is the only country that has more registered cars than people.

67.

The colors of the ITALIAN flag are all represented in the **Margherita pizza** : **basil** for green, **tomatoes** for red and **mozzarella** for white. It was created to celebrate the unification of ITALY in the **19th Century**.

68.

In **1985**, during the hijack of a NORWEGIAN domestic flight, the armed man accepted to trade his gun in exchange for a can of beer.

69.

It can snow in the **Sahara desert**. It happened **three times** since **1979**.

70.

Archeologists found **coins** and **jewellery** on the site of **Stonehenge** in the **UK**, suggesting that it was already a **tourist attraction** during the **Roman Empire**.

71.

Every year, **Munich Airport** in **GERMANY** has its own Christmas market with over **40 stands**, a **50 ft. (15 m) Christmas tree** and even an ice rink.

72.

The most expensive camping spot in the **world** is the **Clayoquot Wilderness Resort** in **Vancouver Island, CANADA**. A single night costs **$3,900**.

73.

The **Great Wall of China** wasn't built in one go. It actually took over **two thousand years** for a few **Chinese dynasties** to finish it.

74.

AOMORi, JAPAN is the **CiTY** with the biggest annual snowfall with more than **312 in. (7.9 m)** on average.

75.

In **AUSTRALiA**, you could visit a **new beach** everyday for **27 years** without ever going to the same one twice.

76.

Dust from the **Sahara Desert** regularly reaches the **Amazon forest** which is **3,000 miles (4828 km)** away and even acts as an essential fertilizer.

77.

St Peter's Square serves as a border between **ITALY** and **VATiCAN CiTY**, making it one of the most beautiful borders in the **world**.

78.

The longest **train** journey in the **world** links **PORTUGAL** to **VIETNAM**. All in all, it's a **10,500-miles trip (17,000 km)** that crosses **12 countries** in about **14 days**.

79.

South Dakota in the **UNITED STATES** has **four times more cows** than people.

80.

DAMASCUS, **SYRIA** is the oldest **CITY** in the **world**. It has been continuously inhabited for at least **11,000 years**.

81.

In some **JAPANESE** hospitals, **special toilets** analyze urine flow and can detect urological problems.

82.

Work on **Stonehenge** in the **UK** started about **five thousand years ago**, during the later part of the **Stone Age**.

83.

The **VATICAN CITY** has the power to issue **passports** to its citizens. Funny thing is that the **Pope** always carries "**Passport number 1**"

84.

CHiNA has only **one official timezone** whereas the country spans **five geographical ones**. The whole country is on **BEiJiNG** time (its capital).

85.

In **1995, Choice Hotels International** introduced online booking for their hotel rooms.

86.

Eggs benedict is a dish that was invented by the chef of the **Waldorf Astoria Hotel** in **NEW YORK CiTY**.

87.

The **Great Barrier Reef** in **AUSTRALiA** is the only **living thing** visible from space.

88.

Metallica became the first band in history to perform on all **seven continents** in **2013** after playing a concert in **Antarctica**.

89.

The largest **cruise ship** in the **world** is the brand new (**2022**) **Wonder of the Seas**. It has **2,867 cabins**, **4 pools** and **20 restaurants**.

90.

You can use a **zipline** to cross the **Guardiana river** which acts as a natural border between **SPAIN** and **PORTUGAL**. Even better, when you land, you will be either **one hour** earlier or later because those two countries are on **different timezones**.

91.

Special tape called **speed tape** can be used for minor temporary repairs on **airplanes**. So, don't be scared if you see a **mechanic** put **speed tape** on the **plane's wing** before your flight. It's way stronger (and also way more expensive) than classic duct tape.

92.

For **Songkran**, **THAi** New year, everyone goes to the street for a big water splash battle.

93.

All **Scandinavian** countries have a cross on their flag.

94.

In **TOKYO**, **JAPAN**, there is a **museum** with more than **1,700 rocks** that have the particularity of all looking like **human faces**.

95.

CANADA is home to **62% of the 1.42 million lakes** on Earth.

96.

The UNITED STATES is the only developed country in the **world** without a single legally required paid vacation day or holiday.

97.

52 generations of the same JAPANESE family have been the successive owners of the oldest hotel in the **world** : the **Nishiyama Onsen Keiunkan.**

98.

23 million portions of **Chicken Tikka Masala** are sold in the **UK** every year making it possibly **BRiTAiN**'s national dish.

99.

The **world**'s most expensive omelet is served at **Le Parker Meridien Hotel** in **NEW YORK CiTY**. It costs **$2,000.**

100.

The biggest (by volume) pyramid in the **world** is the **Great Pyramid of Cholula** in **MEXiCO.**

101.

The **Colorado Springs Airport, USA** features a "**pot amnesty box**" for travelers to dump their unused stash of **marijuana** before leaving, no questions asked.

102.

On **cruises**, "**Meeting of the Friends of Dorothy**" is a codename for LGBTQ gatherings.

103.

More than **one-fourth** of **COSTA RiCA** is protected land to safeguard it against deforestation.

104.

When **trains** were first introduced, some people believed that a **woman**'s internal reproductive **organs** would fly out because of its speed : **50 MPH (80 km/h)**.

105.

Some villages in **NORWAY**, **SWEDEN** and **DENMARK** have a one letter name : **Å**, which means river.

106.

Passports have to be made of materials that bend without creasing for better readability.

107.

Less than **two dozen pilots** are certified to land at **Paro Airport, BHUTAN.** Surrounded by **high mountains**, it can only be approached during daytime and with good visibility making it one of the **world**'s most challenging **airports** for pilots.

108.

In **MUMBAi**, a lunchbox delivery service exists since **1890**. The **Dabbawalas** ("one who carries a box") are now a special unit of **5,000 persons** who still deliver **200,000 lunchboxes** every day.

109.

MONTREAL, **CANADA** had the **world**'s biggest **airport** in the **1970s** but it is now almost entirely abandoned.

110.

The **Henn na Hotel** (which means "**Strange Hotel**" in **JAPANESE**) is the first hotel completely run by **robots**.

111.

In **COLOMBIA**, **Caño Cristales** is the **world**'s most colorful **river**. Nicknamed "Liquid rainbow", it can go from yellow, green, blue, black and especially red. Its coloration is caused by an **aquatic plant**.

112.

You can withdraw money at an **ATM** in **Antartica.**

113.

Isla de las Muñecas is an island dedicated to the lost soul of a **young girl.** It is populated by **hundreds of old baby dolls** hanging from the trees. It has become a popular tourist attraction.

114.

Some **Royal Caribbean ships** have a bar where you can be served by **robot bartenders.**

115.

There is an **instant ramen** museum in **JAPAN** to celebrate that **invention**. There, you can learn about its history and taste a variety of **different flavors**.

116.

The longest route for one **train** is between **MOSCOW** and **VLADiSVOSTOK** on the Trans-Siberian Express railway line (**5,777 mi. or 9,297 km**).

117.

The average cruiser gains **a pound a day** because of the unlimited buffet.

118.

In **ENGLAND**, you can visit a **Gnome reserve** with more than **a thousand of these garden ornements.**

119.

The stones for the building of **Stonehenge** came from **Wales**, over **150 miles away (240 km)**.

120.

The tallest mountain in the **world** is actually not **Mount Everest** but **Mauna Kea** in **Hawaii** : it only rises **13,796 feet (4,205 m)** above sea level but extends about **19,700 feet (6,004 m)** underwater.

121.

Dogs have been banned from **Antartica** since **1994** to prevent them from spreading a disease to the **local seals**.

122.

In a very **special building**, there is a table split in two by the **NORTH** and **SOUTH KOREAN** border. Diplomatic discussions are held at that table without any **official** ever having to leave their own country.

123.

The **Nishiyama Onsen Keiunkan** in **JAPAN** is the oldest hotel in the **world** still active. It was opened more than **1,300 years** ago.

124.

Purple dye was historically a very expensive color (more than **gold**) so it's the rarest color on **world** flags. Only **DOMINICA** and **NICARAGUA** use purple on their national flag.

125.

All **cruise ships** sail with a morgue.

126.

The **DOMINICAN REPUBLIC** is the only country in the **world** with an image of the Bible on its national flag.

127.

The **VATICAN** is the smallest state in the **world** with a surface area of only **0.17 square mile (0.44 square kilometer)**. It's the equivalent of **82 American football fields**.

128.

There is a **picnic table** right at the **triple border point** between **SLOVAKIA, AUSTRIA** and **HUNGARY**.

129.

In the town of **BAARLE**, right on the border between the **NETHERLANDS** and **BELGIUM**, there is a **house** with both a **BELGIAN** and a **DUTCH** address.

130.

DALLOL, **ETHIOPIA** is the hottest inhabited place on the **planet**. Average temperatures reach **106°F (41.1°C)**.

131.

One thousand elephants were used to haul the materials for the construction of the **Taj Mahal** in **INDIA**.

132.

The city of **ANGKOR** in **CAMBODIA** was larger than modern day **LOS ANGELES**, making it the **world**'s largest pre-industrial city.

133.

The **Diomede Islands** are **two islands** that are only **two-and-a-half miles apart (4 km)**. Their particularity is that **Big Diomede** is **RUSSiAN** and the **UNiTED STATES** own **Little Diomede.**

134.

Every year, the habitants of **LOPBURi**, **THAiLAND** organize a huge banquet for the **macaques** that live there. More than **4400 lbs (two tons)** of food is prepared to honor the monkeys.

135.

Queen Elizabeth II was the only person in the **world** who didn't need a passport to travel.

136.

There is one **train station** without an **entrance** or an **exit**, only designed with one **small platform** to admire the landscape in southern **JAPAN.**

137.

The **UK** is the country with the longest name. Its official name is : "**THE UNITED KINGDOM OF GREAT BRITAIN AND NORTHERN IRELAND**" which contains **56 characters.**

138.

The Port of **MIAMI** is the busiest cruise port in the **world**. In **2016**, it welcomed **4.8 million passengers** embarking on a cruise in the **Caribbean sea.**

139.

Every year, **CHiANG MAi**, **THAiLAND** organizes a giant floating lantern festival.

140.

The **Schengen Zone** is an agreement made between **26 European countries** to allow free travel to all their citizens in the area.

141.

42 buildings in **NEW YORK** are so big and receive so much mail that they have their own zip code.

142.

In a **plane**, humidity level is dryer than in the **Sahara desert**. You are basically flying in a **sky desert**.

143.

In **NiCARAGUA**, people don't point with their finger but with their **lips**.

144.

Both **NORTH** and **SOUTH KOREAN** armies choose their **toughest looking soldiers** for a constant stare down contest across the **border**.

145.

FRANCE is the most visited country in the **world**. It welcomes more than **89 million tourists** every year.

146.

In **VENEZUELA**, it is rude to show up on time at an appointment as it could be seen as being too eager or greedy.

147.

There are more than **41,500 airports** in the **world**.

148.

Sandy Island, AUSTRALiA has been on maps for centuries but when scientists tried to reach it in 2012, they find out that it didn't actually exist.

149.

When we think of the pyramids, we obviously think of EGYPT which possesses 138 of them. Surprisingly, SUDAN, another African country, has even more (255).

150.

The largest Spa Resort, the Mission Hills Haikou, is in CHiNA. It is 1.5 times larger than Manhattan island.

151.

To say "no", **BULGARiANS** nod up and down. To say "yes", they shake their heads from side to side. Very confusing.

152.

The "OK" sign used in **North America** by curling the thumb and forefinger together is actually an obscene gesture in **BRAZiL**, **GERMANy** and **TURKEy** and can even be interpreted as a threatening gesture in some parts of the **Middle East**.

153.

In **CHiNA**, you should always leave something behind **on your plate** otherwise **your host** may think they haven't fed you enough.

154.

LiECHTENSTEiN and HAiTi created identical national flags without knowing it. They only realized when they competed against each other during the **1936 Summer Olympics**.

155.

Around **4% of all the cheese** made in the **world** gets stolen at one point.

156.

Since the **U.S.A** started to print **banknotes**, a unique company called "**Crane and Co.**" has been the **paper** provider.

157.

The **city** with the longest name is "**Krung Thep Mahanakhon Amon Rattanakosin Mahinthara Yuthaya Mahadilok Phop Noppharat Ratchathani Burirom Udomratchaniwet Mahasathan Amon Piman Awatan Sathit Sakkathattiya Witsanukam Prasit**" (**163 letters**) but you'll agree it's easier to pronounce its other name :**BANGKOK**.

158.

The total length of the **Great Wall of China** is **13,170 miles (21,195 km)** but contrary to popular belief, it can not be seen from space with the naked eye.

159.

MEXiCO CiTY is unfortunately sinking at a rate of about **15.7 in. (40 cm)** per year.

160.

The **North Pole** is not actually on land but on a giant block of ice floating in the ocean.

161.

Taking a **vacation** can lower your risk of heart disease.

162.

NORWAY and **NORTH KOREA** are only separated by one country (**RUSSIA**). Go ahead, check on a map.

163.

Just **6000 years** ago, the **Sahara desert** was a rainforest. Can you imagine ?

164.

"**El Palacio de Sal**" is a hotel in **BOLIVIA** made entirely of **salt blocks**. **Guests** are forbidden to lick its walls to avoid their degradation.

165.

As of **2022**, **JAPANESE** people have the **strongest passport** and can enter **193 countries** without a visa or with a visa on arrival.

166.

On the **Bidasoa river** which separates **FRANCE** and **SPAiN**, **Pheasant island** has the particularity of changing its nationality every **six months** since **1659**.

167.

In **1987**, **American Airlines** saved **$40,000** by removing exactly **one olive** from each salad in First Class meals.

168.

Bali celebrates its **New Year** in absolute silence. The whole **island** shuts off all sounds and lights during one day.

169.

The **Louvre** in **PARiS** is the most visited museum in the **world** with around **10 million visitors** per year.

170.

Hill tribes in **SA PA**, **ViETNAM** have been meeting at "**love markets**" for decades, making it an early form of **speed dating**.

171.

Loudly slurping your **noodles** in **JAPAN** is a sign of politeness.

172.

GERMAN people have the word "**fernweh**" which can be translated by "**far sickness**". It is used to designate an intense urge to travel.

173.

Wales in the **UK** has the railway station with the longest name in the **world** : "**Llanfairpwllgwyngyllgogerychwyrnd-robwllllantysiliogogogoch.**

174.

The smallest **museum** in the **world** is in **NEW YORK CiTY** and is a converted **36 square feet (3.34 square meters)** **elevator shaft**.

175.

The **U.S.** Postal Service can only deliver **mail** and **food** in the **Grand Canyon** by mule.

176.

Sticky rice was used as mortar to build the **Great Wall of China**.

177.

In **ICELAND**, it's very common to let **babies** nap in their strollers outdoor, even in **winter**.

178.

Two million stone blocks were used in the construction of the **Great Pyramid of Giza** in **EGYPT**.

179.

America got its name from **Amerigo Vespucci**, a cartographer from the **15th century**.

180.

You can find **Queen Elizabeth II** on bank notes and coins of more than **30 different countries**. She has been featured on the currency of more different countries than any other person in history.

181.

From the year **2000** to **2013**, some **two hundred cruise ship passengers** vanished without a trace while aboard a **luxury vessel.**

182.

Angle Inlet is an unmanned **U.S.-Canadian border** crossing where you talk to the **custom officer** via a **videophone** and hold your passport up for the **camera.**

183.

You can see a hidden representation of the **Northern lights** if you put the **NORWEGiAN** passport under a **UV lamp**.

184.

More than **50 pieces of luggage** are lost every minute by airlines around the **world**.

185.

Some **cruise ships** have **virtual balconies** made of a **giant flatscreen** in their rooms instead of windows.

186.

It takes over **an hour** to wind the clock of **Big Ben** in **LONDON**.

187.

The most remote place on **Earth** is called **Point Nemo** in the **South Pacific Ocean**. It's literally in the middle of nowhere since the nearest land is about **1,670 miles (2,700 km)** away.

188.

Not too far from **PARiS**, there is a village called **Y**.

189.

Jet lag is worst going **East** rather than traveling **West**. It's because it's more difficult for **our body** to advance its internal clock (going to sleep earlier) than to delay it (going to sleep later).

190.

Bird nest soup is an expensive delicacy in CHINA.

191.

You can walk across LiECHTENSTEiN in less than a day. It's only **15.5 mi. by 2.5 mi. (25 km x 4 km)**.

192.

MONOWi, **NEBRASKA** is a city with a population of only **one person**. Elsie Eiler acts as its mayor, clerk but also the cook of the only restaurant in town.

193.

Jigsaw puzzles were invented in the late **18th century** to be used in **geography classes**.

194.

In the **UNiTED STATES**, airlines have a nickname for **dead bodies** they transport : "**Jim Wilson**". It's for the **crew** to talk about them without alerting any passenger.

195.

The border between the UNiTED ARAB EMiRATES and both SAUDi ARABiA and OMAN is not officially defined so cartographers and diplomats draw the line at their best estimate through the desert.

196.

300,000 builders and 6,000 elephants worked for the construction of Angkor Wat in CAMBODiA.

197.

In RiO DE JANEiRO, BRAZiL, people go to the beach and jump over seven waves while making seven wishes for the new year.

198.

FRANCE's longest border is surprisingly with BRAZiL (**453 mi. or 730 km**).

199.

Angkor Wat in **CAMBODiA** is the **world**'s largest religious structure, spanning **400 acres (1.6 square kilometer)**.

200.

The **EGYPTiAN Pyramid of Giza** is the last of the **seven wonders** of the Ancient World still standing.

201.

The buildings of the ancient city of **Petra** in **JORDAN** are aligned with the cycles of the sun.

202.

OYMYAKON in **RUSSIA**, is the coldest permanently inhabited place on **Earth**. In **1924**, it recorded a record low of **-96.16°F (-71.2°C)**.

203.

Travelers can head to **Terminal 2** of **SAO PAULO**/Guarulhos International Airport in **BRAZiL** to visit its **in-house dentist**, who offers cleaning, whitening, and other dental services.

204.

It is illegal to bring **foie gras** to **INDIA**.

205.

On **Easter Island**, **CHILE**, nobody knows exactly how they moved the **massive statues** called **Moais**.

206.

In **2005**, The ship **Spirit** from **Seabourn Cruise Lines** was attacked by pirates.

207.

Phone chargers are the most common item left behind in **hotel rooms**.

208.

The **Swiss Guard** protecting the **VATiCAN CiTY** wear uniforms that have hardly changed since the **17th Century**.

209.

Eskimos use **refrigerators** to stop their food from freezing.

210.

In **Exumas Island (THE BAHAMAS)**, a local species of **pigs** enjoy swimming with tourists in the sea.

211.

Freedom of Panorama is a special **copyright law** that allows you to take **photographs** and **video footage** of **buildings** permanently located in a public place.

212.

Banana is a popular **pizza** topping in SWEDEN.

213.

In JAPAN during rush hours, railway station attendants push passengers into the **trains** to reach maximum capacity.

214.

Passports are designed to remain readable by machines in temperatures between **-10°C** and **50°C**.

215.

The **Diomede Islands** are a pair of islands very close geographically speaking but split by the international date line so there is a **21-hour timezone difference** between both **islands**.

216.

On **cruises**, "**Friends of Bill W.**" is a codename for "Alcoholics Anonymous".

217.

There is a temple in **Rajasthan, INDiA** where people feed and worship more than **20,000 rats.**

218.

It takes **three months** to clean all the windows of the **Burj Khalifa** skyscraper in **DUBAi.**

219.

NEW CALEDONiA, VENEZUELA and **SLOVENiA** are the only countries in the **world** currently protecting more than **50% of their land** turning them into **national parks** and **wildlife refuges.**

220.

The most colorful country flag is **BELIZE** with **12 different colors**.

221.

The **Carnival Mardi Gras** is a **cruise ship** with the **world**'s first rollercoaster on board of a **boat**.

222.

Passengers using the **Daocheng Yading Airport** in **CHINA** are warned that they could experience dizziness due to the lack of oxygen because of the altitude. At **14,471 ft. (4,411 m)**, it is the highest civilian **airport** in the **world**.

223.

It took **37 years** to build **Angkor Wat** in CAMBODiA.

224.

DENMARK has the oldest flag still in use. It was created in **1625** and its design has not changed since.

225.

In the UK, there are **one or two wedding proposals** at Stonehenge every month.

226.

The gardens of the **Burj Khalifa** skyscraper in **DUBAi** are watered using recycled condensation from the **air conditioning system.**

227.

Known as the "**VENiCE of Africa**", **GANViÉ** is the **world**'s largest village entirely built on stilts (**13 square miles or 34 square kilometers**).

228.

In **1947**, the **Roosevelt Hotel** in **NEW YORK CiTY** was the first hotel to put **televisions** in their guest rooms.

229.

The **Moais** on the **CHiLEAN** **Easter Island** are not only **big head statues** but have bodies buried underneath.

230.

SOUTH KOREA is home to **Haesindang Park**, also known as **"Penis Park"**, a monument dedicated to fertility.

231.

A championship for making the **funniest face** has been taking place in **ENGLAND** since **1267**.

232.

The oldest currency still in use is the BRITISH Pound Sterling. It's **1,200 years** old.

233.

On **Mount Rushmore, 90%** of the carving of the **four UNITED STATES** presidents was done with dynamite.

234.

The FILIPINO flag has the particularity of changing during **war times** when it switches the order of its blue and red **stripes**.

235.

Just off the coast of **CANCUN**, **MEXICO**, you can dive and visit an **underwater museum** made of more than **400 sculptures**.

236.

ICELAND is the only country in the **world** with no **mosquitos**.

237.

600 people work daily at the **Eiffel Tower** making it one of the largest job generating businesses in the **FRENCH** tourism industry.

238.

You can sleep in a **transparent igloo** while marvelling at the northern lights in **LEVi, FiNLAND**.

239.

NORTH KOREA built a fake village with empty buildings lit by automatic timers to try to lure **SOUTH KOREANS** to defect across the border.

240.

Tree trunks were used to form the foundation of **VENiCE**. More than **1,200 years later**, those same trunks still support almost all of the **city center**.

241.

ISTANBUL, **TURKEY** is right between two continents : **Asia** and **Europe**.

242.

It took **one thousand years** to build **Stonehenge** in the **UK**.

243.

In **Catalunya**, **SPAIN**, an essential feature of the traditional nativity scene is the "**caganer**", a bare-bottomed **pooping figurine**. Nowadays, you can even buy a **caganer** of **famous people** as a tourist gift.

244.

Only **five countries** have buildings on their flags : **AFGHANISTAN, CAMBODIA, PORTUGAL, SAN MARINO** and **SPAIN**.

245.

In **GLOUCESTER**, **ENGLAND**, there is an annual race down a steep hill where **contestants** chase **a big rolling cheese**.

246.

The **NICARAGUAN** passport has **89 separate security features** making it one of the least forgeable documents in the **world**.

247.

It took **20 years** for about **40,000 people** to complete the construction of the **Great Pyramid of Giza** in **EGYPT**.

248.

Saint Martin, in the **Caribbean sea**, is the smallest inhabited island divided between two countries, **FRANCE** and the **NETHERLANDS**.

249.

Kansai International Airport, **JAPAN** was in **1994** the **world**'s first **airport** built on an **artificial island**. Unfortunately, it is already sinking due to frequent earthquakes in the region.

250.

The IRISH man **Eamoon Keaveney** has the record of the longest barefoot journey (**1,200 mi. or 2,000 km**). He walked around IRELAND to raise awareness for charity.

251.

Passports became mandatory for overseas travel after **World War I**.

252.

In the **European Alps**, there are a few cross-border ski areas. For example, in the **Portes du Soleil** ski resort, you can ski on the FRENCH side or the SWISS side, no passport needed.

253.

Lake Baikal in RUSSiA is the largest lake in the world. It holds **20% of the global fresh water reserve** in its liquid form.

254.

The AUSTRALiAN **wombat** is the only animal in the **world** that produces **square poos.**

255.

ITALY didn't have any tomato until the **16th Century** so their famous **tomato sauces** are a relatively recent invention.

256.

With **7 lbs (3.17 kg)** per person and per year, **TURKEY** is the biggest consumer of **tea** in the **world**.

257.

NEPAL is the only country in the **world** that does not have a rectangular flag. It's made of **two triangles**.

258.

DUNEDiN in **NEW ZEALAND** is home to the steepest street in the **world, Baldwin Street**, with a slope of **19 degrees**.

259.

In **FRANCE**, people kiss each other on the cheek to say hi. The **number of kisses** depend on the **region.**

260.

In the **1930s,** the **Waldorf Astoria Hotel** in **NEW YORK CiTY** invented **room service.** Its first purpose was to preserve the privacy of the hotel's wealthy and famous guests.

261.

If you quickly flip the pages of the **FiNNiSH passport,** you can see an animation of a **running moose.**

262.

Over **6 million cubic feet (170,000 cubic meters)** of water precipitates every minute over the top of **Horsheshoe Falls** (part of the **Niagara Falls**). To give you a better idea, it's the equivalent of **one million bathtubs** every **sixty seconds**.

263.

The oldest country in the **world** is **IRAN**. Its sovereignty started in **3,200 BCE**.

264.

AFGHANISTAN has the **weakest passport** with only **26 visa-free** or **visa-on-arrival countries** for its holders.

265.

Before **2020**, the busiest flight route in the **world** was linking **SEOUL** to the **KOREAN** island of **Jeju**. One could board a flight every **15 minutes**.

266.

The **Tijuana International Airport** in **MEXICO** lies along the **U.S.** border and even includes a terminal on the **U.S.** side, making it the only **airport** in the **world** to have terminals in **two different countries**.

267.

The houses of **AMSTERDAM** were built very narrow to lower taxes.

268.

Mandarin Chinese is the most spoken language in the **world**. It has **950 million native speakers** and **200 million** learn it as a second language.

269.

There is a **museum** that only accepts really **bad art** as submission in **DEDHAM**, **USA**.

270.

GENOA's Airport in **ITALY** makes one exception to the **100ml** of liquid rule for **pesto**, which goes through a special scanner.

271.

SAMOA switched from driving on the right side to the left in **2009** because it was cheaper to import **left-sided cars** from **NEW ZEALAND** than **right-sided cars** from the **UNITED STATES**.

272.

It reads like the beginning of a joke but a **sheep**, a **rooster** and a **duck** were really the first **hot air balloon** passengers in **1783**.

273.

There is a store in **Alabama** where you can buy items found in unclaimed **airport** baggage.

274.

If you have gained or lost a lot of weight, you may need to renew your **passport**.

275.

For them not to risk being sick at the same time, a commercial **airplane pilot** and their **co-pilot** must eat different meals.

276.

The clock of **Big Ben** in **LONDON** is very accurate, it has only a **two second** delay every **two weeks** .

277.

TOKYO, **JAPAN** with its **37 million inhabitants** is the **world**'s largest city.

278.

Modern cartographers often include **fake towns** called **paper towns** into their **maps** in order to detect future illegal copies. It's called a **copyright trap**.

279.

You can predict the weather by looking at **airplanes**' white trails in the sky. Long trails are early indication of a storm.

280.

There are only **four main passport colors** : red, blue, green and black.

281.

AMERICA's first **steam locomotive** lost a race to a **horse** but still convinced Americans that **trains** were the future of traveling.

282.

The modern use of a **passport** as a form of identification was introduced by **King Henry V** of **ENGLAND** in the **15th century**.

283.

Three thousand years after his death, the **EGYPTIAN** government had to issue a passport for the mummy of **Ramses II** to be able to send it to **FRANCE** for some restoration work.

284.

In the **NETHERLANDS**, people tend to congratulate the whole family for **birthdays**.

285.

The **world**'s biggest **tomato throwing fight** takes place on the **last Wednesday of August** in **BUÑOL**, **SPAIN**.

286.

Singapore Airlines is the second largest buyer of **Dom Perignon champagne** in the world.

287.

The **world**'s largest atlas is the **Earth Platinum**, a book published in **2012**. Its dimensions are **5.9 ft. x 4.6 ft. (1.8 m x 1.4 m)** and it weighs **330 lbs (150 kg)**.

288.

TUVALU, situated halfway between **Hawaii** and **AUSTRALiA**, is the least visited country in the **world** with around **2,000 visitors** per year.

289.

In the PHiLiPPiNES, **Vulcan Points** is a very special place. It is an **island** within a **lake** on an **island** within a **lake** on an **island**.

290.

The RUSSiAN **Alexey Vorov** claims he has hitchhiked a total of **1.2 million miles (2 million kilometers)** from **1977** to this day.

291.

It's considered rude for **passengers** to not ride in the front seat of **taxis** in AUSTRALiA.

292.

There are two FRENCH sentences on the cover of the BRiTiSH Passport : "**Honi soit qui mal y pense**" (Shame on he who thinks evil of it) and "**Dieu et mon droit**" (God and my right).

293.

The beach of **BARCELONA**, **SPAiN** was artificially created for the **1992 Olympics**.

294.

Abraham Lincoln's assassination made **train** travel popular because the **Pullman car** that was used to transport his body got on the front-page of many newspapers at the time.

295.

Mount Everest summit is right in the middle of the border between **CHINA** and **NEPAL**, making it the highest border in the **world**.

296.

Gifting a **knife** to someone in **CHINA** can be misinterpreted as wanting to cut ties with them.

297.

The **Eiffel Tower** needs **130,000 lbs (60 tons)** of paint every **7 years**. The paint job takes **2 years** to complete.

298.

Scientists are still not really sure about the purpose of **Stonehenge** in the **UK**.

299.

A total of **1,443 couples** simultaneously renewed their vows onboard three **Princess Cruise ships** making it a **world** record.

300.

The **PERUVIAN** region around **Machu Picchu** is not a natural habitat for **llamas**. They were purposedly brought there by the **Incas**.

301.

LAS VEGAS is the city with the biggest number of hotel rooms (**over 150,000**).

302.

Big Ben is actually not the name of the famous tower in **LONDON** but the nickname given to its bell. The tower's real name is the **Elizabeth Tower**.

303.

Until **2015**, the border between **INDiA** and **BANGLADESH** was very complicated. There was a third order enclave : a part of **INDiA** inside a part of **BANGLADESH** inside a part of **INDiA** inside **BANGLADESH**.

304.

Singapore Airlines equipped some of its **planes** with a special **cupboard** to respectfully store any unexpected **dead bodies** during the flight until they land.

305.

The longest continuous international border is **the U.S.-Canadian border (5,525 mi. or 8,900 km)**.

306.

In **PERU**, **Incas** built **Machu Picchu** without using any wheel since they didn't have that technology.

307.

There are only two sovereign countries with square flags : SWITZERLAND and VATICAN CITY.

308.

At **Chicago O'Hare's International Airport,** an **airplane** takes off or lands every **37 seconds**.

309.

INDIA is the biggest consumer and exporter of chili peppers in the **world**.

310.

Even if you are not crossing any border, you can get a **special commemorative passport stamp** at two famous tourist spots : **Machu Picchu, PERU** and the **Easter Island, CHiLE.**

311.

In **THAiLAND**, people usually eat with a **fork** and a **spoon**. They never put the **fork** in their mouth but use it to put food onto the **spoon** that they then bring to their mouth.

312.

In **Hawaii**, instead of a traditional postcard, you can mail a **coconut** to your friends. The coconut is free of charge and you only pay for postage fees.

313.

In **CROATiA**, you can visit the **Museum of Broken Relationships**. Anyone who experienced a bad breakup can leave a personal object with a small written explanation.

314.

Only two countries have flags that look different on each side : **PARAGUAY** and **SAUDi ARABiA**.

315.

A natural gas vent in **IRAQ** is called **The Eternal Fire** because it has been continuously burning for over **4,000 years**.

316.

The town of **WYCOMBE**, **UK** weighs its **mayor** every year. If they gained weight during the year, it's "evidence" that they've been living too much off tax payer money and everyone boos.

317.

Over **830 languages (12% of the world's total)** are spoken in one country : **PAPUA NEW GUINEA.**

318.

The **Gevora hotel** in **DUBAi**, with a **height of 1,168.96 ft. (356.33 m)** is the tallest hotel in the **world**.

319.

In the **UK**, **newlywed couples** freeze the top-tier of their **wedding cake** and eat it on their **first anniversary**. It is supposed to bring luck to their marriage.

320.

Changi airport, **SINGAPORE** hosts a butterfly garden with more than **1,000 free-roaming specimens**.

321.

If you undergo face surgery or get a face tattoo, you'll need to renew your **passport**.

322.

Every building in **Machu Picchu**, **PERU** was designed to be earthquake-proof.

323.

A species of **deer** in **GERMANY** still doesn't cross the border where the **Iron Curtain** once stood even though that border has been physically removed more than **20 years** ago.

324.

In **EGYPT**, adding **salt**, **pepper** or any other **spice** to the dish you are eating is considered an insult to the cook.

325.

Smiles were banned on **passport photographs** in **2004** to help facial recognition technologies.

326.

The **Great Wall of China** is the longest **structure** ever build by humankind.

327.

The **CHINESE** were the first to invent **paper money** in the **11th century CE**.

328.

In **ENGLAND**, it's possible to visit a **poison garden** which houses about **100 poisonous plants**.

329.

In **Yunessun Spa Resort**, **JAPAN**, you can soak yourself in giant baths made of **green tea**, **coffee**, **red wine** or even **sake**.

330.

The **Concorde** and the **TU-144** are the only **two commercial airplanes** to ever fly over **twice the speed of sound**.

331.

In FiNLAND, a wife carrying race is organized every year testing the strength of both husbands and marriages.

332.

Over **250 languages** are spoken in **LONDON**, making it the most linguistically diverse city in the **world**

333.

The ENGLiSH and later the U.S. standard railroad gauge (space between both **train** rails) derives directly from the width of **Imperial Roman war chariots** which was approximatively the width of **two horses' asses**.

334.

The **world**'s tallest tree is a California redwood nicknamed **Hyperion**. Over **380 feet (116 m)** in height, its location is kept secret so people would not destroy it.

335.

The **Great Ocean Road** in **AUSTRALIA** is actually the largest permanent war memorial in the **world**.

336.

You can visit a very special house entirely made of **100,000 newspapers** in **Massachusetts, USA**. No smoking allowed inside.

337.

In the middle of the **COSTA RiCAN** jungle, you can sleep in a **Boeing 727** transformed into a **hotel room.**

338.

BRiTAiN has "**ghost trains**" (**trains** without passengers) that run on a redundant route at least **once a week** just to fulfill the legal obligation to keep these routes alive.

339.

BANGKOK is the most visited city in the **world** with around **22.8 million visitors** per year.

340.

ICELAND's territory is growing at the rate of **two inches (five centimeters)** per year due to tectonic movements.

341.

On **Carnival Dream**, a big **cruise ship**, passengers eat about **28,000 shrimps** every week.

342.

It's almost physically impossible to open an **airplane** door mid-air. Don't believe everything you see in action movies.

343.

The first map to put **North** at the top is from **KOREA** and was created in **1402**.

344.

The shortest **passenger flight** is between **Westray** and **Papa Westray** in **SCOTLAND**. It only lasts around **one minute**.

345.

An Iranian named **Mehran Karimi Nasseri** lived in the departure lounge of **Terminal 1** at **Charles de Gaulle Airport, PARiS** for **17 years**.

346.

In **ROMA**, **ITALY**, all the coins thrown in the **Trevi fountain** are collected and given to charity.

347.

When the **ship**'s **crew** has found a **prohibited item** in a **cruiser**'s luggage, they usually summon them in what they call the "**Naughty room**" for an interview.

348.

In **Singapore's airport**, you can admire the **world**'s tallest indoor waterfall (**131 ft. or 40 m**).

349.

The **Eiffel tower** was hated by **Parisians** at first.

350.

The **oldest known map** is a map of the stars painted in the **FRENCH** caves of **Lascaux**. It is approximately **16,500 years old**.

351.

You can ride the **Hogwarts Express** in real life, the **West Highland Line** runs from **GLASGOW** to the port of **MALLAiG**.

352.

TORONTO's **Pearson International Airport** has trained **birds of prey** to keep other birds away. It drastically reduced the **number of bird strikes** with **airplanes**.

353.

According to a study by **Hostelworld**, **UK** travelers are on average the ones who visited the most countries (**10**), followed by **GERMANS** (**8**) and **AUSTRALIANS** (**6**).

354.

Majority of **toilets** in **Southeast Asia** are equipped with a **water gun** instead of toilet paper to clean yourself. It's disturbing at first but very efficient.

355.

There is a therapy pig at **San Francisco International Airport** that helps travelers calm down before their coming flight.

356.

There is a **fake border crossing attraction** in a **MEXiCAN theme park** to dissuade any **potential migrant** to actually cross the **real border.**

357.

SERBiA makes the most expensive cheese in the **world** called **Pule cheese. A pound (453.5 g)** costs over **$1,000**.

358.

There are a lot of ways to represent **our world** on a map. The most popular one, with the **UNiTED STATES** on the left and **Asia** on the right is called the **Mercator projection.**

359.

In **POLAND**, there is a village called **Zalipie** where **flowers** are painted on all the buildings.

360.

The **twinkling lights** of the **Eiffel Tower** at **night** is a work of art protected by **copyright laws.**

361.

On the **Californian** side of the **U.S.-Mexican border**, there is a town called **CALEXiCO** and on the opposite side of the border, a town called **MEXiCALi**.

362.

Nearly **97% of the world population** speaks just **4%** of all the **6,500 languages**.

363.

The country with the most islands in the **world** is SWEDEN (**260,000**).

364.

In **JAPAN**, **trains** are so punctual that you can get a delay certificate to show your employer if your **train** was more than **five minutes** late.

365.

There is a **Toilet Theme Park** in **SUWON**, **SOUTH KOREA** built around the history and culture of **toilets** around the **world**.

You can really help me with this simple thing

Dear **readers**,

As you may know, I write and publish all my books myself. My goal is to show that it's possible to reach the quality level of traditional publishers and even go beyond.

If you enjoyed **this book** *and want to support my work, the best thing you can do is to leave a* **review** *on* **Amazon**. *It will only take 60 seconds and by doing so, you'll actually make the book more attractive to new potential readers.*

Thank you for your help.

Join the Mothership !

If you like my **books**, there is a big chance you'll like my **newsletter**.

You'll regularly receive **special fun facts**, links to **articles** I found really interesting online and even **quizzes** to test your general knowledge.

I'll also keep you updated on new book release and free book promotion events I will be running.

So let's join the **Smart Impact Mothership** !

To **sign up** just scan this **QR code** −>

or simply type this URL :
smartimpact.space/ newsletter

Made in the USA
Las Vegas, NV
30 November 2022

60521827R00075